I0476361

How to Quit Your Job

Escape Soul Crushing Work, Create the Life You Want, and Live Happy – *Second Edition*

By Cyrus Kirkpatrick of www.cyruskirkpatrick.com
(Freedom Based Work Strategies and Adventure Travel)
Copyright 2014 C.K. Media Enterprises L.L.C, All Rights Reserved

Cyrus Kirkpatrick
Lifestyle Design Series

Special Message: Thank you for your purchase of "How to Quit Your Job". I try to maintain quality in the production of my books. This is because of a disappointing trend in the self-publishing world where cheap, outsourced books are mass-produced by marketing firms. They are often unedited or with poor grammar, yet are passed off as real products. It's up to both readers and writers to keep the market quality and spam-free.

Free Supplemental Booklet: Right now you can check out www.cyruskirkpatrick.com/subscribe and receive a free copy of a booklet **"11 Steps to a Free Lifestyle".** For those of us who desire liberty and sustainability, this is an important resource to have alongside this book.

Table of Contents

Introduction

A pessimist sees the difficulty in every opportunity; an optimist sees the opportunity in every difficulty. - Winston Churchill

Welcome to the second edition of "How to Quit Your Job!" by CyrusKirkpatrick.com. I hope that this book reinvigorates your sense of purpose and life strategies concerning your career.

As part of the second edition, there's a new chapter, **Chapter 10: Internet Fallback Jobs**. I've also packed new content into several existing chapters, including a new section in chapter two.

One thing I will ask of you is if you found this book during the free promotional offer, **you can really help me out and give back by leaving a review after you finish reading it**. I thank you in advance for your support.

One more thing: **Amazon assigns the starting point that you begin reading this book.** If you didn't see the table of contents and opening page, please click the back button now.

Enjoy! Let's get started.

First of all, this is not a feel-good self-help book. The purpose of this book is to hit you upside the head with necessary lifestyle changes that you must make IF you are presently unhappy with your financial, career and lifestyle choices.

If you are a person who feels imprisoned in their current situation, complains of being a **"wage slave"**, and feels continuously unsatisfied—this is the program for you, because it's a path out. It's also a book designed to help the chronically unemployed, and those stuck between jobs with no way out.

This book also tackles the how-to methods of finding a new career, jump-starting your professional life, and finding employment in an environment that the media claims is unkind to job seekers.

If your job has eroded your sense of liberty and has left you feeling miserable, then it's time to take a long hard look at what is keeping those shackles around your ankles. This book will help you to examine this situation and seek new answers.

However, do keep in mind that doing something as drastic as quitting your job may jeopardize loved ones who are financially dependent on you, and therefore such decisions must be taken with great care and responsibility.

Continue reading after a careful self-assessment of your life situation. If you are seriously considering terminating your employment and finding a new path in life, understand that this book is designed for you. But do not make any sudden, impulsive decisions without careful consideration of your situation.

It's Possible, Folks

The greatest problem facing mankind is an emotional, spiritual and mental one—it's the crisis of people who are forced to work without living up to their true potential. The switch is very simple: either you're working through your spirited, inner burning fire—or you are doing something that is gradually draining your life away.

It's very possible to work in such a way that you are invigorated every-day. I've seen it before. I've done it. The switch is real, you just have to find where that switch is located.

We are all different, and we are built with unique talents that manifest in a myriad of incredible ways. However, we are NOT the experts of ourselves—and the consequence is that we sometimes don't know what we really want.

Case in point: myself, the author of this book. I have a few core passions, but doing menial tasks at a computer is NOT one of them. Nonetheless, I trained myself to work in website creation and video post-production because my logical mind told me "it's easier to find jobs this way, Cyrus, and you have to be REALISTIC..."

As it turns out, I gave myself horrible advice. I actually like being around people, socializing, and getting sunshine, which these talents don't always afford. I love writing and filmmaking, too. But, I just can't grow old in front of the flickering blue lines of an LED computer glow shining against my face. I can't even write books forever, either. I'd take a job bartending if it meant interacting with people once in a while.

I also learned I don't like negative people. High-stress careers where everybody is pushing each other down to get on top is NOT my idea of a good time. Rather, it's a spiritual antithesis of what I need in my life.

Finally, I know I don't like horrible bosses. As it turns out, terrible managers tend to dwell in the cubicles of those high-octane jobs where new victims—I mean employees—come and go from a revolving door of firings and resignations while some reincarnated Roman Emperor reclines with glee from his $500 Aeron designer office chair.

So, if you're reading these first couple of pages from an Amazon preview, please take note of the following: if all you're going to get from this book is one piece of advice before you close the window—then accept wholeheartedly what you REALLY want, because it's not as hard as you think to make money doing what you love.

With Vision, You Can Do a Lot of Crazy, Crazy Stuff

As I write this passage I am currently traveling Southeast Asia. A few months ago, I was part of an exclusive trip into the depths of North Korea. Before that, I had been working in documentary film production. I've partied in places like Bel Air and Monaco, lived in France, traveled in Italy, created a small local TV show, and plenty of other adventures.

I won't be so brazen as to consider myself "successful". Complete financial independence with an Oscar on my shelf might warrant this title, but I can safely say that I lead my life in such a way that I aim to do what I want to do, while maintaining enough income through independent means that I've rarely had to worry about the idea of going back into the corporate world.

This is not to say that the corporate world is bad, however; the best part about leaving your job is that it opens up new possibilities, including the chance to become a freelancer and promote yourself, which is something we will explore in more detail in this book. However, it also offers you the chance to enter a whole new field; to redefine yourself, change your career and be part of a corporate system that you like versus one that makes you feel miserable.

To read this book is an important first step, because you need to fill your brain with information from a great variety of resources, until you begin to change your natural way of thinking. Before we begin this program, it's important to realize just how sponge-like we humans are—in the sense that we become what we continually expose ourselves to, whether this involves people, attitudes, philosophies, or jobs.

The first step on your path is to realize this, and begin consciously exposing yourself to resources, materials and people that reflect the lifestyle you want to lead, so that as a sponge you're absorbing enough "right stuff" to make the changes in your life that you need.

A New Movement

Thanks to the digital age, more and more people today think like I do. I'd be lying if I said this was the only book on the market that touches on such themes. I believe this is happening out of necessity as people no longer tolerate dead end lifestyles and insufficient job security has left people disillusioned by the middle class dream.

Let's face it, folks. The middle class is drying up, and most jobs are being flushed away like toilet paper. Pencil-pushing careers are now being digitally replaced in every industry, and marketing is more often outsourced to contractors. The size of companies is shrinking while their owners get richer.

Those who maintain their employment may find the quality of their jobs have deteriorated, such as lower wages and a new icy demeanor by the boss. This happens when you no longer have utility (usefulness) and the company is waiting for the next series of lay-offs to get you out of their hair.

I'm skeptical that the mass layoffs over the last five years are only because of the economy. The dreaded "economy" is just a friendly, neutral and hard-to-argue reason to "trim the fat" and introduce the new less-is-more business model.

In fact, sometimes I'm skeptical of the true veracity of the recession.

"Less-is-more" really means replacing your ass with a robot or a guy in Bangladesh. Fewer people scampering around the office means fewer headaches on the upper management and more bucks in their pockets.

Nobody wants to rely anymore on the old fashioned employee / workplace dynamic. This means you have to change with the times, and begin finding creative ways to make money independently. The good news is that this can also be extremely liberating, and this book is going to show you how to do it.

The Independent Contractor Marketplace

In this new "less-is-more" era of business, there is a silver lining. By adopting the attitude of simplification in the business world, you can begin marketing your own services as the simplistic solution for companies who are stingy about bringing in new employees.

For instance, one major industrial construction client of mine outsources all of his business' marketing to local professionals for quick video or photo campaigns without ever employing a full-time office rat. This saves money, while it opens up jobs for freelancers like me (and perhaps you).

While freelancing can be a LOT of hard work, especially as you carve your niche, it's interesting to consider how it is becoming much more standardized. Without a strong freelancing economy, it would be harder to pack a lunchbox and escape from your office. However, at least with today's job market, you'll know there's some freelancing options available if your dream career is still far away but you have to pay the bills in-between.

For these reasons, right now is the best time to do it. We are now going to begin exploring not only the ramifications of leaving your job, but the keys to successful independent contracting.

Chapter 1. Understanding your Priorities

Why is it that you want to leave your job?

Is it your rude co-workers? Your boss's passive aggressive personality? The uncertainty of whether you'll be fired or not—and a desire to just get it over with? Perhaps it's the high stress and long work hours?

While these are major factors to consider leaving a job, the most important thing you should be evaluating within your employment situation is what types of experiences it's lending to your life.

The reason is because experiences is all we are, and it's all we can be. **Nobody on their deathbed has ever said "I should have worked more at the office".** At the end of the day, marginally higher or lower levels of income does not matter unless you're an extremely compulsive shopper and you demand luxury living space. What matters is how you feel about the places you've been and the things you're doing. In other words, if you feel unsatisfied due to a monotonous daily routine, this is a great reason to think about leaving.

We will perhaps see a future where it is common for people to desire experiences over cash, because the illusion that money can fill a void in one's life is fading. In contrast, a brand new experience is the actual thrill. Whether being part of a movie production, climbing in the Andes or just living on your own terms and taking a Salsa class in the evenings—doing your own thing is a much better goal than helping somebody else live *their* dreams—and it also makes a lot more sense than the blind accumulation of money without purpose behind it.

Don't be mistaken—the paradigm behind this book is not that the accumulation of money is somehow bad, but it's that you need to clearly develop a purpose behind the work that you do.

For many of us, the purpose is simply to survive—to make enough "ends meat" to pay rent at the end of the month. But to really succeed and live independently, it's necessary to expand beyond this surface-level goal and to begin considering how to make substantially greater income through an inner-fire and a burning desire to achieve a specific outcome with a set of experiences you absolutely must fulfill.

It's not up to me to tell you what your financial goals should be, but if it involves a better house, better TV and a better car, you may want to carefully consider the direction your life is going, and whether these goals would truly make you happy or not.

Without a concrete vision of where you want your life to go, it becomes much harder to rip yourself away from your existing lifestyle, confront fear and insecurity and emerge from your cocoon. In addition, if your goals are surface-oriented, it's hard to motivate yourself with the passion and fire that you need to really take off.

For example, if the "end-game" of your success is a giant flat-screen LCD TV on your wall, you may find the amount of work it required to achieve this was not worth the final prize (a huge-ass piece of hardware that you have to insure). This could lead to demotivation and a dampening of your ambition.

If, on the other hand, for the same cost of the TV you decided to spend a month in Tahiti learning to surf and meeting beautiful locals—the memory of the experience will last a lifetime, and you'll feel more compelled to succeed further and accomplish yet another awesome experience.

The point is that whatever your goals are in life, you have to figure out your priorities. This means knowing what you truly want, unrelated to society's views of what success is all about. In addition, your goals should not be related to your need to impress people around you. All these desires are fleeting, and if you do achieve a superficial ambition based on social criteria—you'll eventually hate your accomplishment anyway!

Start evaluating this stuff. Open up a Wordpad document right now and start jotting notes down. Ask yourself what makes you afraid of starting new and from scratch. Ask yourself what boiling, unfulfilled desires are in your heart that you want to express through work and career.

If you realize it's time to let your job go, but it's the fear of failure, loss of income or a blow to your ego / status that's holding you back, then you must remain stalwart with the philosophy that failure does not exist; but is merely an alternate of success that helps you to grow and refine your vision to ultimately take things to the next level without trepidation or regret.

Liberty or Security?

Benjamin Franklin famously said that those who give up liberty versus security deserve neither. His quote has a deeper, philosophical point beyond the political spectrum. In your day-to-day life would you personally take security over freedom? What about in your professional life?

Many people in the modern world lead lives of security and dwindling freedom. Ironically, even the "security" is something that is lackluster at best, as working class jobs are often systems that only allow you to scrape by a bare minimal lifestyle—while such meager privileges are continually threatened to be taken away from you. Whether you spend 60 hours a week at Wal Mart or you're an office keyboard pusher, most of us know what this is like.

My first experience with our modern system scared the shit out of me. Back when I was in college I took a year off to work odd jobs, earn some money to deal with increasing debt, and rethink my major. This simple "time out" period resulted in an existential crisis—the same that many young men and women experience when the threat of financial inevitability begins to loom over them. Although temporarily painful, in retrospect this was an important awakening for me.

This was the crossroads where I witnessed many people in my life settle for unsatisfying lives. Because of recession fears, I watched friends and acquaintances abandon college and opt for semi-permanent jobs in places like restaurants and coffee shops. They were never making enough money to get by, and most complained of not reaching their full potential.

These same people once had high-hopes and grandiose visions that ranged from directorial debuts in film-making, achieving Ph. D's, becoming lawyers, to expanding careers in art, photography, or other aesthetic pursuits.

I realized I was drifting along their same path of non-action.

Simultaneously, the "golden handcuffs" did not seem like a wonderful alternative. The guys who "made it" were often just as miserable in their Lexus's and middle-class houses, with early white-hair, stacks of bills, screaming children, and high-stress jobs.

While some people achieve the "American dream" with a modicum of happiness, I've met far too many NASCAR dads and soccer moms who spend every extra breath in their lungs discussing their desire to escape and fulfill some early childhood or college goal that long ago they deprioritized.

Then, through travel, Internet forums, and a lot of exploration, I started to meet people whose lives were congruent with their desires. Whether passionate promoters and DJs at ritzy nightclubs, backpackers in youth hostels, CEOs of startups or non-profit workers making a difference in the world—I experienced a taste of what it's like to do be congruent with your career and personal ambition.

I knew this is the way it had to be.

Today, I work on a daily basis to avoid joining the majority; and to vigilantly resist against the tumults of mediocrity—and this involves aggressively pursuing what I love to do, and forming mental callouses against any type of negative influence that could sabotage my plans.

End of Chapter Exercise: Figure out Your Sleeping Career

Leaving your job behind is the beginning of a new opportunity and also the first step on a scary, unknown path. However, the more FIXED your vision is of what you want to accomplish, the easier this journey is going to be.

This exercise is designed to help guide you on the path of understanding what your priorities in life should be.

For this exercise, you are going to take a weekend doing something that you find absolutely exhilarating. Is it skiing? Painting? How about Paintball? Maybe writing books is what you find amazing, and you can create mystery novels without even trying.

Maybe you just like to have fun, party, and go dancing.

Do you remember the Wordpad document I had you start writing on earlier? Open it back up again, chronicle your experiences indulging in your hobby, and start taking steps to think about how you can rise up to an expert status and turn such a hobby into a career.

Even without formal schooling in the field, I am willing to bet you have a "sleeping career" hidden somewhere that is waiting to reveal itself. If you can begin to discover what it is, the process of leaving your job will be so much easier.

Chapter 2 – Factors to Quit and How to Do it

One of the first things you must do is assess your current work environment, and decide if it's time to make a serious change or not. And then, you must assess yourself, and develop the proper mental groundwork to be able to let go of your employment situation.

From bullying bosses, disconnected management, to mind-numbing repetition and slashed salaries, there are a number of reasons why your job may go from "tolerable" to "get me the hell out of here!"

On Bullies, Toxic Offices, and Other Reasons to Quit

Very often, in the working world our lifestyles are governed by the all-powerful principle of fear. A workplace dominated by fear, aggressive supervisors, and a culture of negativity is most certainly an environment you are justified to escape from.

First, it should be noted that fear and stress is a natural part of anyone's professional life. The most common type of fear I call **internal fear** or **common job fears** because it's the natural anxiety that accompanies any type of job—whether flipping hamburgers or investment banking. This fear is internal; our natural anxieties that accompany any type of performance related activity.

As studies have suggested, a modicum of fear in the workplace boosts productivity.[1] In truth, *fear* of a particular negative outcome has given me enough drive to accomplish some very big goals. A

---

[1] http://www.zerohedge.com/contributed/2013-09-07/fear-increases-productivity-and-old

good manager understands this, and will not lessen the presence of natural job fears, and may work to keep employees understanding the severity and the importance of their tasks.

But the more toxic type of fear is **manipulated fear**. This is when a sense of fear and unease is purposefully created and exploited by external forces in an effort to amplify your existing anxieties to levels beyond any type of reasonable limit. An example of this could be a boss who threatens to fire a subordinate simply as a method to "motivate" him or her to work harder.

From mild pushing, to sadistic workplace bullying, management that attempts to manipulate the emotions of the workforce is a ticket to a very unhealthy environment.

To identify whether or not your emotions are being exploited, let's consider the different types of anxieties we naturally experience on the job, and then we will identify the techniques that could be used to heighten these feelings. The following are some of the common job related worries that most of us deal with every day:

COMMON (NORMAL) JOB FEARS AND STRESSES

- Anxiety of job loss, being laid off.

- Inability to "read" one's supervisor, paranoia that you've upset him or her.

- Anxiety of displeasing or angering a customer or client.

- Performance based anxiety: "Am I doing a good enough job?"

- Peer-based competitive feelings: "Am I doing as good as John / Jane?"

- Fear of stagnation—not being promoted, not being recognized: "Does my boss recognize how hard I worked this week?"

MANIPULATED (TOXIC) FEARS AND STRESSES

- Warnings from corporate headquarters of potential lay-offs even when it's not true.

- Unrealistically high demands in regard to quotas—and the implied threat of firings if the goals are not met.

- Pressure to perform unsafe work in hazardous conditions.

- The continual threat of demotion or status loss within the company.

- Feared created because of a boss who exhibits unpredictable, childish, or even dangerous personality traits.

- Personal attacks used against a worker (insults, degrading remarks, condescension).

- Conscious exclusion (the development of cliques and the purposeful ostracizing of another worker).

CASE STUDY: Amy's Baking Company

In 2013 an episode of "Kitchen Nightmares" with Gordon Ramsay went viral across the Internet when two pathologically disturbed restaurant owners were discovered at an upscale restaurant in Scottsdale, Arizona.

One of the reasons so many people became infuriated after watching the episode is because the cameras caught one of the owners—Amy—firing a young waitress for having the audacity of asking her manager a simple and non-hostile question.

This type of behavior may be utilized on purpose by sadistic bosses as a method of scaring the remaining employees into a state of submission and hard-work.

While ABC is an extreme example of a bad job, some could say the viral phenomenon struck a chord with many people who are terrified of ending up in such a fear-based, hostile work environment. Amy's Baking Company today remains a paragon in popular culture of the type of job to run away from.

The dark side of the working world is that fear is an excellent tool for pushing an employee into a state of submission. Bullies in the guise of supervisors are not hesitant to use Genghis Khan tactics on their little office-empires in an attempt to exert managerial superiority. This can occur anywhere from the cubicles of a software firm to the kitchen at a Denny's.

Other times, fear is cultivated from much higher positions—such as a company's corporate headquarters—through monolithic orders that are detached from your own day-to-day office flow but influential enough to maintain pressure on the entire workforce, usually in an attempt to enhance productivity. An example of this could be a completely absurd sales quota that sends the managers into an insane flurry.

The high amount of fear associated with the majority of jobs and the stress created by manipulative managerial techniques is, I believe, a major factor in the mental health problems of our culture.

If you are in such an environment, and attempts to address the problems do not work, it may be time to call it quits.

It should be noted not every work situation is a negative one. Some of the most successful companies in the world incorporate very positive environments to minimize the amount of general malcontent among the workforce. And, if your plan is to find new employment, these are the companies you must find–whether by word of mouth, reliable online reviews, or by visiting the workplaces yourself and observing the moods of the workers (see chapter 9 later).

But one thing that nobody can predict is whether a new work situation will remain positive and conducive to a healthy mind and lifestyle, or if a monster will come out of hiding. As the 2011 movie "Horrible Bosses" parodied, it's easy for a great situation to turn sour very fast. For instance, if your boss suddenly kicks the bucket and his coke-fiend son inherits control of the company.

Or, more commonly, you are transferred to a new department and your positive environment changes when you receive a new supervisor who matches all the characteristics of a bully, and your office becomes a toxic place to spend your life.

The reason we must be subjected to these fear-based environments is because most companies possess no type of metaphysical filtration system for those who receive power. An individual's success in a company may be more related to their ability to manipulate their superiors into promoting them versus an adherence to mature, leadership-oriented behavior.

In fact, many times a bosses' lack of ethics is attributed to their success much more-so than the cultivation of positive personality traits. In many companies, a snarling drive to reach the top and a numbers-above-all-else attitude are the things that can plant a corporate rookie into a middle-managerial position.

And then you're stuck answering to this person. At which point, it may be necessary to pack up and go.

The Consequences of Bullies

Many of us feel forced to endure the challenges of corporate life, including the sometimes unfriendly personalities that accompany it. However, increasing research suggests the health hazards of tolerating such situations.[2] And, in addition to this statistics by Zogby have shown that 37% of all workers in the United States have reported being bullied on the job.[3] This is an incredible amount of stress and mental duress that many people must endure.

The effects of stress can lead to countless health problems including high blood pressure, heart disease, and even cancers. When one considers our high-stress lifestyles combined the bad food we eat, it becomes no wonder there is so many diseases in the world.

Workplace bullying and terrible management should not be endured. No matter how virtuous you think your stalwart nature is, it won't do any good if the stress catches up to you with mortal consequences.

Fear Based Management Undermines Respect

Researchers at the University of Columbia, Canada[4] conducted research into the managerial type that they classified as the "dominant" leadership personality, and determined that extremely dominant bosses "bully their way to the top", resulting in higher positions of power and higher incomes.

---

[2] http://www.workplacebullying.org/individuals/impact/physical-health-harm/

[3] http://www.workplacebullying.org/wbiresearch/2010-wbi-national-survey/

[4] http://edition.cnn.com/2013/01/03/business/bully-work-prestige-dominance/

Yet, at the same time, the study determined that too many "dominant" managerial techniques undermine the happiness of the workers. Although this study failed to look into the long-term consequences of fear-based management, it's easy to predict how these workplaces evolve.

I once witnessed a small franchise company fall to pieces as a result of the boss using only fear-based, bully-like behavior on his subjects. The large amount of dissatisfaction led to virtually no respect for the boss and the gradual dissolution of the entire staff.

Because he earned no respect, when the time came that this small office required the employees to "bunker down" and tolerate payment delays and other issues, few desired to stay as there was no loyalty toward him. I was the first to leave, followed by our saleswoman a month later. Soon, the office was empty.

This particular boss had used bullying behavior to motivate his saleswoman to achieve a great deal of success, rising to among the highest raw sales data of any franchise in the entire multi-national company. Meanwhile, her day-to-day lifestyle was crippled with high-stress and growing resentment.

At the end of the day, the impressive sales sheet made little difference as the boss was on such bad emotional terms with the woman that she had no motivation to ride out a rough patch and tolerate the management's abuse. Facing unemployment is typically a better option than dealing with a job that simultaneously disrespects you while failing to pay you.

The fate of the company was not so good. With three main positions in the tiny office gone, the franchise fell into disrepair. This is an important moral lesson in management, and how those bosses who replace authentic leadership qualities with excessively dominant behavior and psychological manipulation are creating companies that have temporarily high-numbers, but long-term failure.

And it also shows why you should never tolerate working in such a liberty-sucking environment. Even if you adopt the stoicism of a cow standing in a rainy field and endure the situation, the odds are your boss's little office empire will be as extinct as the Romans in a few years' time.

Other Reasons Your Job Sucks

Aside from bullies, there are plenty of other situations when a job is beyond repair, and where cutting it off becomes your only option.

Ronald Riggio, Ph. D wrote an excellent article in *Psychology Today* about the signs of a toxic work environment.[5] To paraphrase, the erosion of the human element, the increase of bureaucratic red tape, out-of-touch management as well as the festering of bully behavior (discussed previously) are the most well-known work-place killers.

In addition to potentially incurable office factors, many people find themselves simply discontent with a job that lacks a fulfilling purpose. Complacency in your job, a sense of monotony, and a feeling of disappearing inertia can also weigh on workers who otherwise desire some sense of advancement in their lives.

If you feel you will be doing the same pencil-pushing until you're on a cane, and there's no opportunity for advancement, then the odds are you'll be more successful in the long run if you allocate your resources toward a new job—or your own company—where you have the ability to advance.

---

[5] http://www.psychologytoday.com/collections/201106/change-your-job-change-your-life/5-warning-signs-deteriorating-workplace

Evaluate Long-Term Benefit

If you haven't already done so, it's time to consider what the long term goals of your job are.

Hopefully after the Chapter 1 exercise, you had a chance to evaluate some of the things that you really enjoy doing. What you want to do is compare your long-term future in both respects. Evaluate the risk / reward for each pursuit.

Examples:
Open a ski lodge versus achieve an upper management position in sales.
Ski lodge goal: *Long period of finding financing, low income, eating Ramen noodles.*
Management position: *Lots of more cash, buying a Corvette.*
Ski lodge goal: *2-3 years before completion,* ***Management position:*** *indefinite, I have no idea if my boss will ever promote me or not.*
Most importantly, consider your psychological health.

Ski lodge goal: *Promote positive work environment, be my own boss, do work that invigorates me.* ***Management position:*** *will remain in my same workplace for the rest of my life, which makes me feel stressed and depressed. Heightened responsibilities in a company I don't care about.*

You may come up with different answers, and find pursuing your dream career would be MORE stressful than leaving a job that you actually feel OK about.

Or, perhaps you'll realize the long-term benefit of your current job is just not that interesting, at all. It's up to you to discover how you truly feel.

How to Actually Quit Your Job

If by this point you've evaluated other options well-enough, then it's time to consider really doing it and submitting your notice.

In the first edition of this book, I received feedback from readers that they wanted more concrete ideas about the steps required during the actual resignation process. So, now I'll elaborate a bit on this.

The first step is to obviously finish a program like this one **and have concrete post-job plans**. Your unemployment benefits will only go so far. **If you're caring for a family, don't quit with anything less than a reserve of 6 months income**.

Furthermore, there are really two routes to go: **quitting or being fired**. Depending on your tactic, if your job has been experiencing mass layoffs and you feel you're next, **it might be a good idea to wait until you become one of the casualties.**

The reason is simple: **severance pay**. You won't get any if you voluntarily resign. If, however, your company decides to make you resign, you'll typically be entitled to a good severance package.

This is also why it's important to go over the stuff you signed when you joined the company. Analyze the handbooks or manuals you may have received when you were hired, examine the severance agreements, and make sure there are no discrepancies to what you will actually receive.

After the layoff occurs, it's important to negotiate the situation with your boss and ask if there is flexibility. There is no hurt in trying to seek a better severance pay.

Most companies pay about 2 weeks pay per year of your employment. So, if you've been working for 5 years, you should be entitled to 10 weeks severance payment.

Some more things to negotiate include:

- Bonuses: if you were due for a raise or a promotion, factor that in. If your pay was originally going to double, you should get paid double in your severance.

- Health benefits: see if you can get extended medical coverage.

- A positive reference: This will help you with future jobs, should you seek further employment by others.

Quitting Versus Being Fired, And Unemployment Benefits

It's important to note that **without adequate reason for quitting, you'll most likely receive no unemployment benefits**.

If you're living in the United States, these laws vary on a state to state basis. **There are some situations where you can contest this.**

While it's best to consult a legal professional in this instance, here are some basic factors that might help your case.

- If your work environment is very hostile, including threats aimed against you.

- If you have previously filed complaints to any state business office or regulatory agency about your workplace issues.

- If your workplace is unsafe or hazardous.

- If you are deemed psychologically unfit to continue working, or experience any other medical condition that prevents your ability to work.

- If you have to quit to care for a family member.

Your case will also be greatly helped if there is evidence to support your grievance, especially by any type of regulatory agency (especially in regard to hazardous working conditions).

In situations where the workplace is hostile or abusive, a history of misconduct, police reports, and / or successful lawsuits filed against your company by former employees may help you.

For U.S. residents, to reach your local unemployment office, try going here: http://www.servicelocator.org/OWSLinks.asp.

Not Getting Screwed On the Way Out

There are some instances when an employer may hand you a bunch of things to sign as you leave. This could occur during a voluntary resignation or during a layoff.

Don't sign anything. Even if you hear a lot of verbal sleight-of-hand, like "can you sign this stuff as protocol? Thanks!".

In reality, **they could be making you sign non-competition agreements**. What this means is that they don't want you to work within your industry ever again. They're afraid you'll go to another job in a competing company, or create a business using some of their ideas.

If you need to hire a lawyer at this point, you may need to go this route. An especially aggressive company may try to coerce you into signing something, either by threatening to withhold severance benefits, or claiming that you already entered a contract whereby you're forced to sign a non-competition clause.

For this reason, you should also be very mindful about anything you signed, or any documents in your possession, from when you first joined the company, or anything you may have signed at any point during your tenure.

There may be laws in your state that prevent companies from coercing employees. I would again suggest to consult with a legal professional.

Leaving Without Benefits

In many situations, like the ones I've outlined in this book, a workplace may become very toxic, but you have no basis to earn benefits simply for quitting.

In this case, how well you succeed at quitting your job is entirely up to how much prior planning you've performed.

You need to evaluate, very hard, your current expenses and liabilities. Understand that resigning may take with it lost lifestyle benefits. This may include your car, toys, insurances, vacation plans and even living quarters.

The purpose behind this book, and the rest of the chapters that follow this one, is to help establish your plan, so that you have the option to resign without being lost at sea.

Starting a business can be a frantic process, and figuring out your goals and personal entrepreneurial ambitions can take months of soul-searching. Use this book as a resource to help with that, **and avoid resigning in a heat of passion**.

You need a plan, you need a strategy. If you give up one morning and yell into the ceiling fan that you're renouncing the world and it's evil ways; you might feel empowered, and you might empower some of your other co-workers, **but without a plan you might end up on food stamps and living with your parents again.**

Two Important Pieces of Advice

No matter the situation, be mature. Throwing a fit or being disrespectful may hurt you in multiple ways, even if your employer deserves to be tossed from a window.

Firstly, you may lose later allies. Remember, you're still a professional, and your company is one of the industries that understand the best. Some of your co-workers or even managers could one day be your employees or business partners.

Secondly, it can cost you severance benefits and / or even unemployment benefits. They may even be able to create a legal case against you if they can prove you were an abusive employee.

So be polite and control your emotions. **Remember your job is not your identity**. We'll be reinforcing this concept throughout this book. As a result, quitting or being fired should not have to bring out uncontrollable emotions.

The second piece of advice **is to use a concealed digital audio recorder at all times, hidden on your body, if you're in an especially weird / hostile / bizarre work environment.**

This may give you a huge legal advantage if your crazy employers try anything wacky on your way out; such as threatening you or using any type of coercion against you.

Hey! Wait! Person reading this! Yes...You!

Do you have a copy yet of the free booklet that goes alongside "How to Quit Your Job"?

It's called "11 Steps to a Free Lifestyle" and it's designed to help round out your education in your new Freedom Based Work Strategy.

Just go to www.cyruskirkpatrick.com/subscribe and enter your e-mail and I'll send it to you.

After you sign up, I'm also available to answer any questions you have. Like, I'll help you with problems you're having if you e-mail me with advice about your business or lifestyle plans.

That's like, free consultation. I have way too much time on my hands.

Chapter 3 - Independent Income Strategies

There are many ways to find a new career or earn money; from early retirement to finding work abroad. However this book focuses in particular on the independent income strategy—the ability to work for yourself, preferably regardless of geographic location, to allow the most amount of freedom possible as you create a new career for yourself.

There are several ways that you can establish independent income:

- Establishing income as an independent contractor and develop your own clientele.

- Creating your own company with effective management philosophies to lessen workload and ensure a non-toxic environment (so that you avoid going into a soul-crushing work experience all over again, or creating it for others).

- Achieve personal expertise in your career and professional recognition to expand your network, sell products, or earn royalties.

- Earn passive income to remove work from the equation.

The four work-life strategies are all potential angles, and it's up to you which one best suits you.

It's necessary to make note of the passive income route; as this is one of the more popular work-life paradigms. It involves the ability to take "work" out of the picture altogether by accumulating wealth through an autopilot system, and spending your free time pursuing the things you love to do.

My opinion is that before you even begin to think about automating your business or reducing the hours you invest per week, you must first determine what type of independent work will keep you continually interested and with opportunities to advance your career, and then you have to spend a very long time using one of the other 3 models to create a profitable industry that works before you can outsource the help and create an automated system.

Therefore, I wouldn't recommend beginning your venture into independent finances with automation as a short-term goal. I've seen this desire blindside people. The truth is, building something new is going to take a lot of hours at your laptop, at trade shows, and generally doing work-stuff.

However, if passive income is the thing you absolutely want immediately, there is many books related to this topic available on Kindle, including of course Timothy Ferriss' famed "*The Four Hour Work Week*". Just be wary of the supposed easy path. If your potential company involves a dynamic, changing market—you have to stay ahead of the game, and working 4 hours a week won't suffice against competition.

Fueling Your Work with Vision

If you don't have any lofty desires like exploring the ancient ruins of Petra in Jordan, or taking a hot air balloon ride across America, then take this time to remember what it is you really want to do in life— the odds are you've simply forgotten the things you always wanted to do as a kid.

It's this type of desire that you can use to your advantage to push yourself through the slow periods of your new career. Whenever you feel a lack of motivation, you can practice visualizing the places you want to see and the experiences that you want to have. This will keep your motivation levels high.

You Need Consistency

How well you accomplish tasks related to your new venture is about ONE principle: can you accomplish things even if you DON'T feel motivated? You might feel pumped one evening, write up a business plan for a mobile company, and search Wikitravel for the ultimate new place to relocate, but unless you can think like this every single night and work on steps consistently, you'll fall behind—and ultimately fall on your face.

Have Fun

Before we begin the next exercise, I wanted to mention what my law professor when I was an undergrad used to say "if you're not having fun, you're not doing it right". That was a hard class, but I got my hardest-earned "A" in college by learning to enjoy it, host study sessions, and absorb the material. I take that lesson with me into work environments.

And it's a lot easier to have fun in a job that's in line with your goals, because then the work never feels pointless. You're building something, and using visualization of the experiences you want to have (Chapter 1) to remind yourself of the things you want to do before you die.

End of Chapter Exercise: Create a Plan of Action

Do you remember your weekend indulging in your favorite hobbies? Hopefully now you've had some time think about how you can take one of your interests and morph it into a new career that can cushion you as you transition from your current employment situation.

If your hobby is skiing—taking up employment at a ski store might be an OK first step, but if you're aiming to think big—then you'll need to do a bit more work than this.

You need to create a "Plan of Action" for yourself. This is like an informal business plan, as it will be a collection of notes related to the marketplace of your selected hobby.

Figure out where the money is at, how you could position yourself into that industry, and how you can expand your talent.

Research can be done easily on Google. There's a professional side to every industry. If it's as something as obscure as collecting glass marbles—there's a bustling industry somewhere that manufactures them.

Next, create a timeline on this document: what you hope to accomplish by when, including when if necessary to finish a formalized business plan to seek investor financing.

In addition, this is where you'll need to pinpoint what your independent income strategy is going to be (mentioned at the beginning of this chapter). Whether it's a brick-and-mortar business or an online enterprise managed by yourself, you'll need to figure out what you're working toward.

Finally, consider how you can give back to the world. This is an important step, as any type of venture created out of purely selfish interests is, in my opinion, eventually doomed. By having a plan to return something to the planet in an honest way, you'll be providing a more genuine service which will ultimately yield more sales.

This outline is for your own reference. Keep it with you, folded it up in your briefcase, and take it out when you have a moment of free-time to analyze your goals, check off benchmarks and brainstorm new ideas.

Chapter 4 - Immediate Action

Speed is the essence of war. Take advantage of the enemy's unpreparedness; travel by unexpected routes and strike him where he has taken no precautions. – Sun Tzu

Strategy is good, as is practice. No matter which of the four strategies that you decide to develop, it's important to make swift decisions to begin expanding your independent abilities.

Almost everybody I've ever met has elaborated on lofty independent goals: "Yes, I'm writing a book. I write about one paragraph a month, but…" or my favorite: "Did you read my screenplay? Someday I'm taking this baby to Hollywood!"

This immature behavior is not sufficient for anybody serious about taking their life to the next level. It's the dividing line between the successful and unsuccessful.

For an example: if you're not serious about turning your screenplay writing into a career, then be honest with yourself that you're writing as a hobby and that you have no intention to make profit from it or become an industry professional. If you lie to yourself, you're burning your own fuel.

If, however, you are serious—then don't do a half-assed job. Write your screenplay and actually finish the thing. Then, invest some money toward an agent or professional editor. Once you've put up your own money into a project, the incentive to see it through until completion and earn your money back becomes very high.

Even if you don't succeed, it's extremely empowering to go from point zero until the creative process is actually completed, with a tangible result. Just holding that finished script in your hand, even if you didn't find a perfect agent to sell it is still a feat that may empower you to find that success later on down the road.

Already in the last chapter I mentioned "life purpose" several times. This is discussed in more depth in the next chapters, but it's important to point out that whatever your goals might be—it's not necessary to have fully imagined them before you start acting on them.

When it comes to making decisions to rectify an unhappy situation, the number one mistake all people make is to delay the necessary progression and postpone immediate action.

Examples of immediate actions you might want to take right now include:

- The title of this book: resignation from your job IF the consequences will not negatively impact other people (child support, for instance).

- Finishing an important part of your career (a certification, a degree, a personal website, etc).

- Ending a toxic relationship with a wife / husband / girlfriend / boyfriend / room-mate, business partner, etc.

- Launching of a personal business.

- Acquiring a new job if unemployed.

- Finishing a major project (a book, a movie, a business plan).

- Any step toward the completion of a major life goal (earning a Ph. D, traveling the world, etc).

Direct Actions are Better than Excess Planning

The amount of strategy and waiting periods for the "perfect moment" should be minimal when it comes to escaping any situation that has entangled your sense of welfare, freedom, or general happiness.

Obviously, you can't just quit your job without careful consideration of the factors involved, and even proper emotional or philosophical preparedness, but if a situation has become irreparably corrosive—something has to be done, and fast.

If your dream is to make money independently and travel the world—you cannot afford to daydream about methods of "how". 80% of your technique to accomplish this should be action, with only 20% toward planning or strategizing. If you find yourself daydreaming too much—snap out of it! Start creating real actions instead.

This means for every ten days you work toward your new path, eight days should be devoted to fulfilling goals, and only two days spent mulling over your ideas, reconsidering options or changing your course of direction.

This could mean immediately seeking an investor to support your business, immediately working on a product, or immediately seeking new types of work abroad. Whatever your goals are, concrete steps are required, while failures along the path should be regarded as little more than hiccups—or better yet—opportunities to change direction.

Identifying Concrete versus Imaginary Steps

INTANGIBLE: Dreaming of ideas for a new book.

TANGIBLE: <u>Opening Microsoft Word and writing the first paragraph.</u>

INTANGIBLE: Writing down thoughts about how much capital is required to start a business.

TANGIBLE: <u>Cold-calling companies, trying to get past the secretary, and pitching your business idea to potential investors.</u>

INTANGIBLE: Considering what finances are needed to learn a specific skill in school to begin a new career.

TANGIBLE: <u>Realizing you don't need to wait for enough money for tuition when you can purchase textbooks on Amazon and start teaching yourself.</u>

You'd be amazed how many intangible actions you're committing. Most of the time, these are intangible because it's really non-action, laziness or fear hiding behind the disguise of "planning", "analyzing" or "being prepared".

You need to nip this behavior in the bud. You could spend hours, days or years analyzing something before taking action. Meanwhile, your competitors have left you in the dust.

This entire phenomenon tends to happen because excess thought and analysis prevents the true physical creation process, which is the only way you can successfully design, compete, and create.

To illustrate this more clearly: the person who writes a 500 page manuscript on how to successfully compete against Dole and break into the fruit business is far behind the guy who's actually on a plantation picking his own strawberries. The person who's out there getting the job done is going to be the first to earn the spoils.

But Should I Really Quit My Job?

Indecision is a painful process, because it traps a person in-between two worlds, and neither world becomes very pleasant, as one's heart is not fully committed to either.

The best plan of action is to consider the practical reasons to stay or exit your current situation, and think objectively about the real consequences if you do go (Will I be unable to afford child support? Do significant others currently depend on my cash flow?).

If quitting your job won't negatively affect somebody else, then you should understand that the idea you'll be some unemployed, homeless bum is a myth. You must have faith in yourself that you will persevere. Eliminate the invalid (fear-based, paranoid) excuses that hold you back, and stride forward even in the face of criticism or the insinuation by family members that you are foolish.

Setting Boundaries

Part of taking action involves setting personal borders as you decide what's acceptable in your lifestyle, and what isn't. This is because it's surprisingly easy to fall back into the same situation as before unless you create limits.

For instance, one such boundary could be: "I will not work under another person in an office-related environment." This is a good boundary to establish if history has shown repeated failures and unhappiness anytime a boss puts you in a cubicle.

It's very important to understand your boundaries and to apply them to your new path. For instance: your dream career path involves working at a video game company. Yet, at the same time, you set a boundary that you will never again work in a traditional office environment. This may create a conflict of interest. You may be allured by the thought of becoming a glamorous, respected game designer, but if staring at a computer screen in a cubicle makes you go crazy, then you had best change your dream career to something more aligned to what you know really makes you happy. Or, find a way to adapt your interest to a different type of work environment.

Likewise, if you have trouble when you work independently, and you need the structure of an office and a good supervisor, you may not have an easy time in a career that involves self-paced work.

Before you go any further in this program, you need to seriously consider your own personality, and what your strengths and limitations are. The more honestly that you can assess your professional capabilities the quicker you will achieve true, lasting success.

Are You Spinning Your Emotional Wheels?

One of my favorite speakers and authors is Dr. Paul Dobransky, author of *The Secret Psychology of How We Fall in Love*. He has written and spoken to a great extent about not only relationship issues but also career topics and what makes human beings happy. In his literature the power of the personal boundary in both relationships and in the professional world are part of his model for a psychologically healthy person.

As Dobransky explains in many of his lectures, a major cause of unhappiness is the spinning of emotional wheels. Many times there are situations we have no control over, yet we obsess and stress about them ad infinitum until we are left miserable.

I've had co-workers and friends who have found themselves in miserable work environments because of a belief they can somehow fix the situation by remaining in the company, or that their impossible to please boss will eventually become satisfied by their work (without any evidence to suggest such a turnaround will ever happen).

Despite the stress from their job spilling into their personal lives, they remain stoic and they endure the situation as long as they can. But, I think this is an example of mismanaged boundaries.

Whether an intimate relationship or a job, if your relation with another person involves impossible expectations and potentially abusive behavior, it's best to accept that there is nothing you can really do to change this person, and trying to expend personal energy to reshape something that cannot be fixed will only create more stress.

End of Chapter Exercise: Immediate Action

It's now time to consider what **tangible** actions can be immediately implemented to begin a better life. It involves identifying, and taking action toward a problem area of your life.

- Write on a piece of paper or type on a word document what parts of your life are damaging your: welfare, sense of freedom, and personal happiness.

- Identify how you are responsible for each negative situation. This is part of the process of taking charge of your goals versus playing the victim.

- Accept your responsibility

- Now figure out at least one tangible action that can help change your path.

- This could be ending a very toxic relationship with someone, eliminating a stressful source of debt, or to stop tolerating your uncle's late-night phone-calls where he screams about politics for an hour as you patiently listen.

Chapter 5 - Taking the Plunge

Bend toward your strengths, lest you break on your weaknesses –
Unknown

At some point, you have to make a decision point. It may involve resigning from your job, or staying. Either way, if your plan is to create some type of independent income, and / or eventually your own business, there's some important first steps to make.

Creating a Business: A Web Presence

Depending on the nature of the "sleeping career" that you've decided to awaken, you can either create a traditional business, a personalized service as a career professional, or a strictly online company.

Regardless, one of the first things you'll want to do is make a presence on the Internet. This will help you attract your first clients or customers, and assist with presentations.

Everywhere you turn, people seem to be making online companies. And, people continually tout the great benefits of making money online. Unfortunately, there's a lot of miasma mixed into the reviews and the hype.

Making an online business is the same as any other type of business, with the difference being that you don't have a brick-and-mortar location to establish shop. Instead, you must rely on the patronage of those who visit your site.

At this point, you may want to consider if the career goals you've outlined in the previous chapters are compatible as an online business or not. However, regardless of whether you're opening a physical ski shop or an e-store, a web presence of some type is still required.

Your biggest challenges will be:

- Finding a market to tap into, or creating new demand.
- Establishing and fulfilling a product
- Website development
- Maintaining traffic
- Optimizing ROI and CTR (Return on Investment and your Click Through Rate.

Briefly this is what you're getting back for the time you're putting in, and how many people are clicking on your website through your marketing efforts, finding your product and clicking "Buy").

Typically, the idea behind an online business is to simplify operations to the point it's possible to run things off the laptop. This is why online businesses are usually small operations with between 1 and 6 people. (Of course, they could also have thousands of employees).

There's an allure to income passivity that sends most people in the direction of creating some type of product that people can click to buy, or a subscription based web-service with customer service handled through an outsourced call-center.

However, both of these business designs require complicated fulfillment models that may require strenuous web knowledge and a lot of upfront cash to get off the ground.

Instead, you may want to consider first doing an actual service that involves physically meeting with clients. While the hands-free attitude of online business appeals to our inner anti-social recluse, the reality is that meeting people face-to-face may be the best way to generate new sales and all-important notoriety as you begin.

Then, after you've performed the service for a while, maybe you can tap into your existing reputation to do things like sell merchandise, e-books or some other affiliated online product to compliment your abilities, and perhaps even switch entirely to that coveted automated income model that I talked about back in Chapter 3.

Redefining the "Niche": Going Where the Competition Is

So how do you optimize your CTR, expand markets and get the business you need to make a company successful? The best way is to ensure you've positioned yourself in a strategic location where competition is heavy yet the demand is heavier.

There is a myth of the niche, and it's the idea that it's necessary to find a unique subclass of people with a specific and odd shared interest to make money. For instance, lovers of Tenor saxophones or fans of Doctor Who. There's a lot of pressure for originality that weighs heavily on would-be entrepreneurs.

My experience in web marketing has proven at least one thing: it's possible to build a fan base for a narrow niche, but hard to get them to spend money. It's easier, however, to figure out where people are spending money, where the competition already exists, and try to improve on what your competitors offer.

Obviously, you want to find a demand in a field related to the dream career you've picked for yourself (see prior chapters). However, if your dream career is very nebulous ("hitting on girls and playing video games the rest of my life…") you may want to refine your search for a marketplace and be flexible with new ideas as you create an actual service.

Regardless of how you do it, once you enter the marketplace you'll be going head-to-head against people who were there first and know the business better than you. This is where most people chicken out.

There are several factors that may allow you to blow up the existing competition, even in a new market you know only a little about. Start researching your competition and take note of the following factors:

- Customer Service: How good do they make people feel?
- Personal Charm: How good do they make people feel?
- Honesty: How good do they make people feel?
- Service: How good do they make people feel?

Notice a pattern yet?

Disregarding these factors will bankrupt you. Period. Businesses die before they hit the ground when a would-be entrepreneur has so much lust for making easy dollars that they neglect the entire process of serving customers and making them feel good.

Fortunately, a lot of people are not properly aligned to those virtues I listed above, which means by practicing good customer service and a mindful attitude, you can become deadly competition against those who don't care. In addition, reasonable prices are a great incentive, too.

Examples of Finding Demand First

No matter what your subject of interest is, you'll find—somewhere—a demand for a service. I would suggest go where the demand is the highest.

In my continual ski lodge example, I would look into the demand of fixing broken pairs of skis. People crash their gear all of the time, and there's a demand for people to fix ski equipment.

If you're starting from scratch, however, there's a lot more options. Figure out what people are searching for and what they need en masse. Instead of looking for a niche, look for a desire that people have.

Many people, for instance, want to learn how to fix things around the house to avoid paying hundreds of dollars to contractors. For this reason, there will always be a demand for how-to guides.

That's just one example—start studying trends and figure out where the money is moving, and move with it.

The Online Component

Another place people get hung-up is the website component of a new business. It's important to think of a website as a giant business card. Even if you hire a great SEO web designer, it's unlikely you'll be in popular Google search terms for a long time, and ultimately it's a site that people arrive at through word of mouth or typing in what they found on your actual business card.

As notoriety builds, you will gain site traffic. Alternatively, you can chip away hours upon hours trying to build traffic through web marketing techniques (and there's a bazillion resources to help you with this, I'd check first with the *Warrior Forums*). You must do this eventually, but I've found it mind-numbing as a first step. That time should be spent performing the actual service, making face-to-face connections, or presenting local lectures to promote a book or product.

The other way to approach the concept of a website is that it's ultimately a flier or sales pitch for your product. In this case, every advertisement you produce will send potential customers to a place where the look, feel, and ergonomics of what they see contributes to whether there is a sale or not.

I've seen people waste thousands of dollars on web-designers too early. You can buy hosting and design a basic site with a Wordpress.org template in under a day's work. If you're completely computer illiterate, hire a student for a few bucks to put one together for you.

As for marketing your new career, you can create business through many ways. The online component includes Google and Facebook ads, which are known as PPC (Pay Per Click), a potentially expensive way to earn your first clients, and which involve a whole science not covered in this book (but there is COUNTLESS resources online to teach you).

You can try blogging and finding strong search engine terms through the **Google Keyword Planner**, but this is a lengthy process that is often outsourced to companies that provide copywriting services.

Or, you can even post ads on Craigslist, put up fliers in select locations, and host lectures about your topic to local community college classes. The point is, however, to ensure you're in the right marketplace. If there's no demand, none of the above efforts will yield any result.

However the best bet starting out, in my experience, is just do what you enjoy and MEET people. Your new career is almost entirely dependent on a zeal to expand your website, portfolio, or network.

Don't rely entirely on Internet marketing for anything you do. There's hundreds of millions of Internet marketers out there. The way to develop your new reputation, and long-term clients, is by getting out of the house and going to any and every function you can so people can put a face behind your online presence.

Hiring Employees

From worker's compensation fees to health insurance mandates, a company with employees saps a lot of resources.

It takes some guts to bring employees into the fray for any type of business. Strangely, I've seen such gutsy people do this very early on, even in businesses that do not necessarily require it. This can damage your startup, you credibility, and any sense of free time that you enjoy.

Many consultants suggest the importance of not "doing everything yourself". This is true, but you can handle a lot through assistance from students in exchange for college credit (or some money), plus outsourced contractors through resources like Elance.com. An actual employee on an hourly wage should be avoided at all costs UNTIL the following conditions are met:

• You have a SURPLUS of net revenue coming into the company.
• You're prepared to LOSE money and the business won't fold.
• You project stability in the company.

Not abiding by these rules means you are creating a condition that is a cardinal sin according to this book: you're creating someone else's terrible job.

A mistake people make is to bankroll a set of employees while holding faith that the company will start generating enough revenue to pay their salaries as a result of their employment in the company. Here's what this strategy results in:

• An over-stressed manager (you) who will probably unintentionally make the lives of the employees into hell.
• The inability to pay your employees.

- Everyone quitting as this occurs.
- Becoming known as someone who can't fulfill promises.
- Endangering the sustainability of people who want to work and are also supporting families and loved ones.

There MAY be some exceptions to this. If you're opening a coffee stand and you want a couple of people to man the shop on a part-time basis as some silly minimal wage gig, and you know enough coffee is flying off the shelf that $8.25 ($11.25 or so after taxes and expenses) per hour is no problem, then OK, hire away.

But do NOT invest everything toward some startup with limited resources, while making promises you can't fulfill as part of an elaborate job description on Monster.com or Craigslist.

Startups are a scary thing for people to work for. It's always on shaky ground, and people don't generally like working for a company that's on the edge of a cliff. Instead do the right thing and plan your business so that you can outsource to affordable independent contractors for the stuff you can't handle early on, and hire employees only after the company is raking in dough that you're able to give back to the community in the form of sustainable employment.

More Resources to Find Demand

There are many resources to figure out what people are interested in, and where the money is flowing. Begin taking mental note of what direction the economy is going, what technology is hot, and what types of products are always needed. If possible, relate these business ideas with your own interests, hobbies, skills and passions.

- Check Google Trends (http://www.google.com/trends/). When you find out what's going (or about to go) viral, you can be ahead of the game with product development. Also check YouTube trends.

- Once again I suggest researching keywords on the Google Keyword Planner. But use it smartly. Pay attention to the media, find out what's trending, and as soon as you suspect a new market is about to appear, start finding out what specific terms people are plugging into Google, and see how such terms could be used to draw attention to your service or product.

- Look for new types of magazines at your local bookstore. Few would invest in the troubled publishing industry anymore unless it's related to a topic that people feel confident will garner sales.

Paperwork and Other Mumbo Jumbo

Not everybody is born with an innate talent to understand everything about business law and paperwork. Instead, you should do two things: read this chapter, and then invest a hundred bucks or whatever amount is needed to talk to a local business lawyer for an hour or two.

The basics are this: you're going to work as an independent contractor, with a company that's probably going to be in the form of either a sole proprietorship, or an LLC which is a somewhat "easy" to configure corporation that has special features to lessen your legal liability.

There is a wide horizon of state specific laws, taxes and fees that apply to your LLC, that require a bit of knowledge beforehand if you choose this path. However, creating an LLC is often as simple as filling out some paperwork at your city's business office. After some initial (hopefully small) fees, and opening a business account through your favorite bank, you'll be good to go.

(Note: Creating an LLC in California is very costly, and possibly other states as well. In Arizona it was nearly free, but when I tried to make a company in Los Angeles I was facing an $800 charge! So, again, check with your business office).

As a sole proprietor, you may not even have to register as *anything*, as this is what you'll be listed under automatically when you file your taxes at the end of the year. However, again depending on your jurisdiction, you may need to file some paperwork.

Many prefer the LLC to the sole proprietorship as it provides greater protection for the day you get a manic bloodthirsty client who wants to sue you (it's happened to me and may happen to you).

Management and Outsourcing

Machiavelli sums up how I feel about outsourcing work:

"Because, if one is on the spot, disorders are seen as they spring up, and one can quickly remedy them; but if one is not at hand, they are heard of only when they are great, and then one can no longer remedy them. Besides this, the country is not pillaged by your officials; the subjects are satisfied by prompt recourse to the prince; thus, wishing to be good, they have more cause to love him, and wishing to be otherwise, to fear him. He who would attack that state from the outside must have the utmost caution; as long as the prince resides there it can only be wrested from him with the greatest difficulty." – Nicolo Machiavelli, The Prince

What Machiavelli is trying to explain is to remain cautious setting up any system that removes you from the equation. It's typically better to be prompt and available, especially as your business is starting out.

Although you can begin removing your own presence and allow others to do the work, it suffers risks of removing both leadership and the vision behind what is making the enterprise work.

For now, learn the system yourself thoroughly before investing money for other people to take over the operations—whether that involves updating your website or dealing with customer service issues.

End of Chapter Exercise: Make a Website and a Business

Whether or not you've decided to leave your job behind, it's always a good idea to go ahead and begin marketing and branding yourself in a way that you can quickly get to work promoting yourself and perhaps finding your first opportunities to make money independently and doing what you love.

There's three essentials that you need: start a business, make a website, and make business cards.

To accomplish these tasks, you'll be taking your "Sleeping Career" you discovered in the prior chapters and positioning yourself as an industry expert in that field. If it's dirt-biking, that's perfect—you'll create a website featuring yourself as a dirt-bike "enthusiast and professional" with business cards to match.

Here's a basic roadmap:

- Go to your local chamber of commerce and inquire about how to start a sole proprietorship or an LLC. You'll handle some paperwork and possibly pay a small fee.

- Read up some basics on making a website. I'd suggest start with a hosting company (GoDaddy, Dreamhost, Hostgator) and purchase Wordpress hosting plus a domain name (yourname.com, johndoedirtbiking.com, etc). This is a way to easily access a dashboard that allows you to upload free templates to have an immediate web presence that doesn't look extremely amateur. As you need more help in this area, you can outsource to students or designers on a freelancing site like Elance.

- Spend an evening writing copy to describe yourself, your experience in the field, and what types of potential services you can offer.

- Synthesize this into a business card. If needed, find some stock images online and add it to your card to spruce it up. Finally, include your website address on the card. When it's designed upload it (or design it from scratch) on VistaPrint.com or a site that's similar.

Now you at the very least have a virtual presence behind your soon-to-be company, and you know some of the basics about the relationship between an independent venture and an Internet presence. However, don't forget my advice about networking in the REAL world. Over at CyrusKirkpatrick.com there are many products in the Lifestyle Design series related specifically to the improvement of social skills and high-end networking.

Chapter 6 - the Secret of Self Discipline

Your dreams can take many forms. Whether you desire to have your own wine company in the Mediterranean, a motor-sports tour company, to make a modest income while you sail the blue ocean, or to become a famous TV actor with a supporting role in a major network series—these ambitions cannot be realized without one very simple concept that can boost any man or woman above virtually all of their peers.

Here is your "magic pill" to success. I hope you're sitting down:

The Secret: To be able to do work when you don't feel like it.

Wait, what?

That's literally the one thing that separates successful people from those who are stuck in one gear.

It's a very basic concept that a three-year-old could teach you, but most of us are ignorant about the relationship between work and personal feelings.

Motivation is a Trap

Motivation is like a burning, fuel-powered engine—haven't you heard people say "You have drive!"?. But the problem with any engine is that it's powered on a limited resource.

Motivation can be a powerful force. The odds are, when you read a book like this one, it pumps you full of it. Then, in a single marathon, you start taking action. In a few days you've taken leaps and strides.

But then, what always happens is that as the motivation simmers down, the original incentive to accomplish such tasks goes away.

Why does this happen? To understand this, it's important to understand human nature. Humans tend to avoid anything that inconveniences them or otherwise takes excessive time to accomplish. We want quick results, and we have shorter attention spans than ever before. In addition, we are constantly seeking the quickest solution that requires the least amount of work.

Diets fail because the vast majority of people are shackled to this behavior. Good luck selling a diet plan with the pitch "Become Thin and Beautiful in 12 Months of Hard Work!"

It's difficult to override this tendency. Somehow it's hard-wired into us, possibly a product of evolutionary psychology as it can be beneficial on a practical level; for instance if we must traverse a long and arduous journey the quicker and more expeditious we can reach our destination, the less risk we will incur of waiting around to get eaten by a sabertooth tiger.

But this impatient behavior sabotages our goals when it's translated into things like career motivation or the desire to change one's lifestyle.

The only way to override this tendency is that you should immediately confront situations where you feel inconvenienced or there is a lack of enthusiasm to accomplish something you know you must finish.

It's this ability that separates a true warrior from the rest of the herd. This is also a concept that has a similarity to eastern philosophy and Buddhist teachings of "Right Action". I call it the "Do it NOW Approach".

This is a powerful concept in productivity that will not only help you launch your business, but begin taking care of things that you may have put off for way too long.

Exercise: Perform the "Do it NOW Approach"

For this chapter's exercise, you are going to immediately begin performing duties that you have either disregarded or forgotten about. You are going to read this exercise, set this book down, and do *nothing* else but focus on finishing your duties. When you are done, you may pick this book up again. If you break this rule, you have failed yourself.

- The first step is to identify what chores or duties you've neglected, put on the "back burner" and otherwise forgotten about.

- It may involve cleaning your room, removing that moldy casserole from the back of the fridge, or finally getting yourself to the dentist.

- Identify a list of ten such things. It's not hard to do—we all have a stockpile of them.

- Mark a number by each task, on a 1-10 scale grading how badly you *don't* want to finish the task.

- Begin performing the *Do it NOW* technique to eliminate the highest graded tasks first. Gauge your own feelings of apprehension, and take note of your ability to override these feelings.

- When the tasks are complete, compare your feelings of elation with your initial feeling of apprehension or fear.

- Almost always, to get something that was nagging your brain out of your head is going to feel *really good*. In the future, identify with that elated feeling in-order to more easily accomplish tasks in the future.

Applying This "Secret" To Your Work

If you liked this chapter's exercise, you may want to conduct these lists more often, and in the context of your business project.

The idea is to adopt a philosophy of self-determination every-day. For me, personally, it was hard to shake off habits like video games and excessive reruns of *Game of Thrones*, but these days I can stay fairly committed to my independent projects without being distracted.

It helps that I do the work that I find exciting, and it rarely feels like drudgery. But, even when it does, I perform the "Do it NOW" method to force myself out of those ruts, pushing past mental roadblocks to progress more rapidly.

Chapter 7 - Escape the Matrix

By now, you've learned the fundamental ideas behind reinventing your lifestyle and career, and the importance of getting out of an employment situation that has compromised your sense of freedom. Now, I want to talk about the bigger picture; the patterns of societal behavior that will always threaten your liberty unless you become aware of them.

The tendency to mimic other people's path and purpose, including general day-to-day decisions, is possibly hardwired into our genes. A hundred thousand years ago, straying too far from your tribe would have dire consequences, such as being devoured by a sabertooth tiger. Naturally, those who were the best at following the chief and copying other people's behavior would never stray from the herd, and would therefore live much longer.

But in the modern age "following the herd" is not so useful, At best, it will keep you in a consistent pattern of behavior—a matrix— possibly long enough to earn a steady paycheck and a bit of security. At worst, you become a pawn used by other, smarter but ill-intentioned people who are aware of the weaknesses of the human personality and the methods to exploit people.

The reason we are talking about this is because a key to being good at business, and successful at life—avoiding exploitation—is to really think outside of the box, and train yourself to become aware of forces around you (whether advertisers, corporations or politicians) that might be manipulating you.

On the topic of quitting your job, sometimes the simple act of waking up to how exploitation works is enough to inspire a person to find new job. I've spent some time living in Los Angeles, and I encountered more than a few situations where Hollywood hopefuls would work 50-60 hours a week WITHOUT pay in the hopes that they will "make it big".

And what happens after their 6 month gig is up? The door is closed on them, and they are replaced by someone younger and better looking. If any of these people I see were aware of how they were being exploited, I am sure they would have taken off their rose-colored glasses and gotten the hell away from those companies.

In essence, individuals, companies and governments thrive on exploitation. It's very important in life to have the wherewithal to recognize symptoms of exploitation and keep yourself from falling victim.

Lessons I Learned in Thailand

Thailand, Laos, Vietnam and Cambodia are all countries that are heavily exploited by foreign multinationals. Traveling in Southeast Asia, I learned about the extent to which these people are used for cheap labor.

One friend of mine from Thailand's rural region of Isaan used to work for a Danish manufacturing company that had outsourced operations. She described her job conditions as "existence as a human robot".

Every woman in the factory had to wear matching outfits, and they were not allowed to converse with one another, not even to say hello. The job entailed repeating the same action, such as adding a piston to a small machine or a computer chip into a clock, hundreds of times per day.

Unlike a company such as FOXCon, the dreaded Chinese slave labor firm, this Danish company took "better" care of their employees. As a reward for working for the company for years, my friend's pay increased to almost U.S. $14,000 a year, and they even purchased a car for her. Keep in mind this is a great sum of money for a rural Thai.

But it made little difference, because her work day was 12 hours, 7 days per week. She had no lifestyle to speak of, barely saw her three kids, and corporate policy prevented her from having friends inside of the company. The money was thus useless to the improvement of her life, although it greatly assisted her family.

Nonetheless, the "golden handcuffs" kept her on the factory floor for a decade. The fear of losing the large monthly paycheck kept her terrified of leaving the company. They paid her just enough to keep her from leaving and manipulated her to stay in a psychologically damaging situation; through the idea that better jobs do not exist for poor Thai people.

It was in a moment of bravery that she realized she was living as a robot. In a few swift decisions she moved south toward Bangkok and the gulf, where there was a surprising amount of work opportunities (with legitimate companies, not what you're thinking!).

Few paid quite as good as her prior robotic existence, but she could afford a normal lifestyle again that included recreation, going to nightclubs, and having friends. The increased spirit and morale has allowed her to earn more money on the side, and provide better care for her family and spend more time with them than during her factory job.

The Tendency for Self Flagellation

Most readers of this book are enjoying the comforts of western civilization, and perhaps feel far-removed from the story I just told, but it's important to understand that it's not uncommon to end up exploited, underpaid, and in a surprisingly similar situation as the

Thai girl, just with a more polished veneer that comes with an American or European lifestyle.

The tendency to follow in the footsteps of others is how so many people end up with dead-end jobs, crushed dreams, and robotic lifestyles similar to my friend from Isaan. All of these five "culprits" are unhealthy ways of thinking that you have to recognize so you do not fall into another soul-crushing employment situation:

Culprit 1: "Work hard, endure a shitty job and get a bigger 401k to someday enjoy the good life".

This has also been referred to as "life deferment". It's why I've met so many unhappy seniors. In reality you can start doing what you like to do RIGHT now. It just requires more work and dedication. Don't wait until you're too old to really enjoy life. Get started during your best years however you can.

Culprit 2: "As long as I make money, I can have a better lifestyle and maybe more chicks will like me".

This is a flawed way of thinking that a lot of men fall into. They maintain a job they hate under the illusion that the status provided will create more attention from women, and then they'll be happy. This is a socially contrived myth that keeps people working for the wrong reasons. Also, women care more about your personality then your job, (with the exception of DJs... Ladies love DJs).

Culprit 3: "I must know my place in society fitted to my diploma. More educated people get better jobs, whereas I am best suited for Arby's".

This is the reason why ninety-eight percent of urbanites from my home city seem to never leave their graveyard fast food restaurant shifts. To have a college degree is an advantage, but it's not a blockade if you don't have one. Most people cite Bill Gates' lack of a completed college education to debunk this. My own degree looks nice on my wall but it has not had a huge influence on my post-college business pursuits. I'd still be doing cool stuff if I hadn't finished college, and you can too.

Culprit 4: "Once I achieve X Y Z, I'll finally do what I want to do in life."

This is self-rationalization and fear of change. You'd be amazed how much can be done this moment without waiting until conditions are perfect.

Culprit 5: "If I become poor, I'll lose status, less people will like me, I'll become homeless".

Here's a very common anxiety. There is no link between large amounts of cash and happiness, and "status" is a completely arbitrary concept. For this reason, many people are scared of giving up jobs they despise because the idea of making less money is terrifying.

The road to success may involve sleeping on a friend's couch for a couple of months, and there's no shame in this. You're only a "homeless bum" if you have no path or direction and prefer to smoke weed and play video-games rather than stay pro-active.

Do You See the Matrix?

Why people's lives stagnate is directly related to the "herd mentality" I first spoke of. The reason a social myth like "I have to wait and enjoy my life after I retire" propagates is because we design our lives based on what we see other people do, not what actually works.

We may also endeavor the mistake of listening to advice from peers or parental figures, who also gain their "knowledge and wisdom" from the same social conditioning. Ever have someone tell you "This is just the way it is in real-life"?. This is the typical rationalization people use for spreading bad advice.

People heatedly defend these points of view because they themselves have subscribed to it, and it's very hard for people to shake off their existing beliefs if they've modeled their lives around it.

Bad Socio-Cultural Memes Are Exploited

Furthermore, limited thinking is used by the more knowledgeable to increase their own material gain.

This occurs most commonly when large groups of advertisers design their next campaigns to sell some product. They tap into socially preconceived ideas about what is cool or status-enhancing *based on notions that they themselves concocted*. They will then reinforce the idea with bold statements and gaudy photography. This is known as hyper-reality.

This influences public perception, and encourages people to live their lives for the wrong reasons. This allows them to spend the money they earn from their dead-end jobs on tools that are supposed to make them happier, and yet sunglasses, cars and shoes never really do the trick, so it's assumed there's something wrong with the consumer—maybe they need *more* until the status enhancement fully takes effect. And so, the pattern of consumerism continues.

Take note I am not ragging on the entire advertising process. In fact, I enjoy advertising, creating ads, and marketing. What IS a problem are our own abilities to decipher advertising from reality. The only time an advertiser is crossing ethical boundaries is in the event of false-advertising. Otherwise, it's the consumer's responsibility to practice critical thinking and not be suckered into false idealisms that lead to financial distress and misdirected life priorities.

Employers Reap Profits

Cunning employers understand what specific mental models will keep people working for low wages with promises of incentives that are never delivered.

One of the methods is by keeping people *believing* that they are not worthy of anything beyond the job they are given, as such low-standards are required in-order to fulfill hard, low-paying positions. This is why manipulative employers like to say: "You're lucky to even have a job!"

A perfect example of this was revealed during the investigation into the abusive conditions at FOXCon. It was revealed how many workers who joined the company as part of student "internships" from across mainland China. The conditions were so terrible that the company reportedly built "nets" around their buildings to catch suicide attempts. The job consisted of extremely long hours with abusively low pay.

This was an exploitation of the "I must trough through the sludge to succeed" mentality that I find prevalent in Asian countries. Somehow, I find it doubtful that the human-machines from FOXCon are going to move up the corporate ladder with fruitful jobs at Apple through their "internship" opportunities.

I've been to China enough times to know that while economic conditions are not very good, a street vendor who sells barbecued pork in Beijing is going to make a lot more money and be a lot happier than the average FOXCon employee who works 18 hours a day and brings home a hundred bucks at the end of the month.

And yet, these same employees were so convinced that they *had* to trough through that sludge that they would sooner plummet to their deaths from the top floor of their factory than simply quit their jobs to go sell barbecued pork or any other way to make independent money. Death was more appealing than the idea of losing face-value and "giving up".

Back home in America, I've discovered similar unpaid internship conditions among students who are just trying to "move up" in the corporate world. Nothing as extreme as FOXCon, but exploitation still happens and you have to remain vigilant and aware.

End of Chapter Exercise: Find Your Purpose

How often do you take time out for yourself to consider your future, and set a forward momentum? These days, it's rare that people leave the confines of their city, living space or social group.

Step 1: Find a remote space, preferably in nature. This may include a local mountain, the countryside, a forest or any other location. If you don't have a car, figure out a bus route.

Step 2: Take out three hours to absorb this location. Focus on the surroundings, the temperature, the fresh air. Make sure your cell phone is turned off.

Step 3: As you begin to relax, and your mind drifts from your daily hassles or stress, think about what things you've accomplished in your life, and why you've accomplished them.

Step 4: Continue to ask yourself "why" questions, as if digging a tunnel. Why did you earn your degree? What do you want out of your current employment? When you hosted that charity event, why did you do it?

Step 5: When you cannot ask "why" questions anymore, you'll have a possible main purpose.

Step 6: Identify secondary purposes. It's OK to have more than one. Personally, I have about three.

Step 7: Try to make the rest of the day a period of relaxation. Don't stress about your problems in life for once. Instead, meditate on your purpose. Wake up the next day and feel refreshed.

In Summary

The lesson is that you have to be aware of your own shortcomings and the very common tendency for people to underestimate their own abilities. Small-minded, socially constructed "matrix" thinking is extremely common, and it's exploited by those in positions of power to get the better of us.

They will perhaps never lose their supply of gullible and cheap labor, as well as people driven by the motivation to become happy through meaningless consumerist habits, but every-day new people wake up and see what's really going on, and realize that experiences are the fruit of life, and that working like a horse to buy some status-symbol like a new car will neither enhance one's happiness nor propel anyone toward a brighter future.

Chapter 8 - Redefining Success

In the last chapter, we discussed socially conditioned attitudes as they relate to consumerism and exploitation. In this chapter, we will begin redefining personal success from a healthy point of view that extends beyond *consumerism*.

This is necessary in-order to pursue your new career from an honest point of view, versus remaining motivated by something flighty and superfluous, like the idea that material success will reap affection from the opposite sex, or any type of half-hearted pursuit of fame or attention with money as the catalyst.

According to psychologist David G. Myers[6], new generations have a greater quantity of *stuff* compared to their parents, yet there is no evidence that we are any happier.

In fact, we are on more anti-depressants and report general dissatisfaction on a much wider scale, while less materialistic people appear largely happier than their counterparts.

Furthermore, the study also determined that those deemed "materialistic" appear to be most miserable with low finances, but when they achieve moderate financial success their happiness level *almost* increases enough to catch up with non-materialistic poorer people, who are naturally more content with their lives.

I think this study begs the question: "What is a materialistic person?" My definition is that it's anybody who desires physical objects above and beyond more sociable experiences with others or immaterial satisfaction, including travel, dinner with friends, a night on the town, or just solitary personal enjoyment.

---

[6] http://www.apa.org/monitor/jun04/discontents.aspx

If financial resources are instead continually allocated to *unnecessary* goods: an upgraded car, a better TV, a new microwave oven—then it's reasonable to say the consumer is materialistic by nature.

The flaw with materialism is that it requires continual resources to maintain happiness. In addition, it sucks away resources by requiring investment toward ephemeral goods that will just need eventual replacement and further costs.

Why Are We Materialistic?

Materialism is a psychological phenomenon that seems married to advertising, and our tendency to identify and emulate the way other people live their lives.

Advertising uses a *false model* of a fictional person's life with which we can compare our own lives to. The happy teenagers bouncing around at the house party and holding plastic cups of some sickly fluorescent orange juice drink is a fictional representation that exploits our tendency to emulate what we think of as successful or high-value behavior.

We then associate our emulated desire with the specific object: the high-fructose corn syrup laden juice drink. The happy teenagers are drinking it, and I want to be happy and popular too. So in-between finding a bunch of young friends with perfect teeth and model-like features, I must also go out and buy the orange juice so that I can emulate the television's representation of happiness.

There is a sliver of truth hidden in the phenomenon of advertising's link to success. On Wall Street, you better have a nice suit if you want to make a good impression, as people will judge you for your appearance and how much you've invested on your clothes, and you may even lose a huge opportunity if you're wearing a cheap suit.

The same can be said if you want to get into one of those trendy Los Angeles nightclubs (although I'm not sure why you'd want to). In this case, those designer shades that you're rocking at nighttime could be the thing that helps the bouncer to decide to let you in, giving you access to various Hollywood celebrities and / or their cocaine dealers.

Therefore, materialism *may* have utilitarian purposes. But in this case, it's not really materialism so much as implementing a strategy that requires the use of consumer goods. True materialism is when a person *believes* the façade that the brand-name piece of nylon or plastic has helped shape their identity. In other words, it's when the guy who got into the Hollywood nightclub actually believes those Gucci sunglasses have made him into some type of baller high-status guy just like on some billboard advertisement. This is when practicality turns into brainwashing.

Such brainwashing is implanted on purpose by advertisers who are experts at psychological manipulation. This type of reasoning creates a very weak psychological blueprint, wherein a person's identity is attached to a piece of plastic, nylon or alloy, and if the artifact is taken away–the consumer's identity is dismantled in the process, thus initiating the purchase of a new object to fix the sense of loss.

A Byproduct of Capitalism

Advertising and consumerism / materialism are things that will always be attached to a capitalist system, and in small doses I don't even think it's that bad. Hell, I feel pretty good when I buy a new shirt, and some of it could be attributed to some polished looking male model dude rocking out the threads on some banner I see when I drive to the store.

However, achieving financial independence requires recognizing the illusions of capitalism so that you do not fall into bad spending habits. If you carry the belief that things like material status and fashion are key components to your happiness, you'll never be able to save enough money to start a new business or income model because you're accumulating $500.00 weekly price-tags on bullshit like Gucci sunglasses and new cell-phones.

Remove the perception that material goods equal happiness and you won't bind your finances to the accumulation of things.

Redefining Success and the Workplace

In June 2013, Arianna Huffington, the multi-millionaire founder of the mega-blogging corporation "The Huffington Post", hosted a makeshift conference in her New York City apartment titled "The Third Metric: Redefining Success Beyond Money and Power"[7].

This small conference, which included famous actors and spokespeople, was an accumulation of years of research into just how unhappy the American workforce has become. At some point in this nation's history, 20-hour work-days, neglecting family to burn time in the office, and coping with horrible bosses versus standing up to them became the unquestioned "norm" and attempts to insinuate that such behavior is bad, unhealthy or even "unsuccessful' has remained completely taboo.

The Huffington Post has addressed some of these issues in their own workforce by providing accommodations like "nap rooms" for stressed out employees to take time-off to unwind. Aside from methods to keep employees from burning out, other factors that increase a worker's quality of life and thus their level of true 'success' include sympathetic supervisors who understand a link

---

[7] http://www.huffingtonpost.com/news/third-metric

between a worker's productivity, and whether or not the employee feels imprisoned by their job.

Huffington also believes that the tendency to separate living and working (a "work life balance") is a misnomer that leads us to resenting our working lives because it separates us from our "real lives" that we are desperately trying to get back to as we count down the clock. One point of the conference is the theory that it's better to ultimately combine working and living into a suitable lifestyle with reduced pain and suffering.

However, the higher-arching theme of this new way of thinking has nothing to do with nap time and management theory, but it's about dispelling an ancient social meme that working like a horse and self-flagellation is synonymous with being successful.

While money leads to flexibility, security for the future and alleviation from temporary problems, a job that saps away personal liberty and leaves that creative supercomputer inside your skull unused and dusty is going to damage your sense of well-being worse than a lack of riches.

End of Chapter Exercise: Become a Hippy for a Week

To detach yourself from material excess, so that you can learn to regulate your finances and be unafraid of the perils of "failure", it's important to separate from your life of affluence for a while.

From being in poor areas of Thailand, Laos, Cambodia, parts of China, and North Korea, I've seen how people have the power to adapt and sustain themselves on bare minimal. By contrast, even the homeless in western developed countries don't experience quite the level of scarcity and daily toil for survival as experienced by the 90% of many of these countries.

And yet, they still survive. Major lessons can be learned from extreme poverty, in particular about maintaining without first world luxuries and discovering your life does not necessarily suffer as a bad as you think.

A major source of "failure fear" is the idea that quitting your job and doing your own thing will make you into a "homeless bum". This stereotype is reinforced by family, friends, and the media. It's the belief that there's a class system in place, and it's easy to slip and fall to the bottom, where you will quickly become a junkie sleeping on the sidewalk.

If you're serious about nullifying these fears and confronting your comfort zone, I'd suggest taking a 'hobo vacation' to experience what it's really like to be on the proverbial bottom of the ladder.

- Pick a place you want to go to. Almost anywhere will work. Including a place you've always dreamt of but are too afraid of the expenses.

- Sign up to Couchsurfing.com, ask around on CraigsList for a temporary homestay, or look into budget hostels in that area.

- Pack bare minimal. The minimal amount of clothes and personal supplies you need to get by.

- If you go through Couchsurfing, you'll be staying in people's houses for a while. It's a great way to meet people, but you must also be prepared to make some lifestyle adjustments.

- A budget hostel may fit you into a dorm room, just like college again. I've never had a bad experience doing, and you won't either as long as you pick reputed hostels through Hostelworld.com.

- You're on a bare minimal budget, so expect to buy very cheap food, do a lot of cooking yourself, and try to avoid old creature comforts like restaurants and excess shopping.

- Learn to adapt to the changes and enjoy yourself in spite yourself. Tally your expenses at the end and discover how cheaply you can get by even in a potentially expensive new location.

I would recommend performing this exercise someplace you've been dying to see, whether it's Venice, Italy or an island paradise in Fiji. Aside from the plane ticket, you'll be spending very little money by planning your vacation this way.

The lessons from this experience will also help teach you about how life is not actually bad without hotels and "luxury". And, in fact, not having much money can even be fun and provide a chance to meet people.

When this is done, I believe you will have a new sense of confidence to take chances and pursue new ventures without fear of losing certain comforts.

Chapter 9 - Returning to the Workforce with Renewed Purpose

The point of this book has been to give you a chance to consider your purpose in life, what things really inspire you, and to help you unplug from socially conditioned behavior that is brainwashing you. In addition, we have gone through necessary steps to help you think of your own business and begin earning money independently.

The end result of these exercises is that you should now be in a much healthier mental state to enter the job market again.

The greatest danger to a man or woman who is seeking a job is desperation. The more desperate you are, the more you'll attract untrustworthy employers who can smell your neediness like a shark scouting for blood in the water.

By positioning yourself as an expert in a field you are passionate about (whether dirt biking, skiing, Polka dancing, whatever you love), you are going to have a deeper sense of confidence regardless of the type of job you enter.

The reason is because you'll now understand that you don't need a position in a company to define yourself, and you have at least some opportunities to make money doing what you love regardless of your employment status or not.

Furthermore, by taking time to consider your purpose in life, you'll be naturally directing yourself toward the types of employment situations that are probably more in line with the things that you want to be doing with your time.

The Trick to Nailing an Interview

As you look for a new job, there is a simple formula that will help you to achieve a lot more success with your job interviews. That formula is honesty + relaxation. An employer with integrity wants to work with somebody who understands his or her own faults. When your interviewer asks about your limitations, this is a good chance to be honest. Never say canned nonsense you read in advice columns like "My biggest weakness is I work too hard".

Always avoid anything that detracts from your authenticity.

As for relaxation, this only occurs if you are not attached to the outcome of the interview. By having an element of independence in your life—whether it's a website or a secondary career—it's easier eliminate that pressure when you already have a strong sense of purpose, who you are, and what you're doing with your life.

Guaranteed, the candidate who appears totally relaxed during the interview process, who does not care if he or she gets the job or not, is going to be (ironically) the winner out of 10, 50 or 500 applicants.

Many programs tell you to relax by breathing exercise, meditation, and so forth. This is all bullshit. The only way you can truly be at ease at an interview is to GENUINELY not care about the outcome.

Take note of this bit of advice because I swear it will change your world forever (it did for me).

Scouting a Terrible Work Environment

Clearly, the last thing you want is to end up in a terrible work situation a second time. To prevent this, ensure the dynamic of the interview process also involves YOU evaluating THEM.

Just like when the role is reversed, the interviewer will typically prop up things up in the best light possible by ensuring you that all of the employees at Acme industries are happy and fulfilled.

And, just like when the role is switched, it's easy to get bullshitted, and this is why background checks are important for both sides. With your prospective new company, evaluate the working conditions; run some Google searches, even contact former employees.

You could even ask to be given a tour of the offices. Pay attention to the dynamics of the workplace; warning signs include employees who are not interacting with one another, grimaces, loud or gossipy middle-management, and any undefined element that gives you a "bad feeling".

If the workplace is a shop or restaurant, pay attention to how the employees treat their customers, and don't apply to a business where you repeatedly receive bad customer service. The reason is because there is a trickle-down effect where bad bosses make employees feel like shit, and they treat their customers like shit in return. 90% of the time bad customer service is the fault of management, not the staff.

Beware of Low Hanging Fruit

Finally, it's very important to dedicate some time to discuss some of the "low hanging fruit" in the job market that you need to RUN from.

Because so many people have scarcity mindsets, and are desperate for work, predators have designed every type of job scam imaginable. In the midst of the so-called Great Recession, they've really stepped up their efforts.

If you're having a difficult time securing interviews or finding places to apply at, this is the best time to be patient versus randomly picking things off Craigslist ads.

Before I list some of the "jobs" to stay away from, I should point out that the cardinal rule is beware of ANY company that is too eager to hire people. Symptoms include lots of repeat Angieslist and Craigslist ads by the same company, or even friends and acquaintances who excitedly tell you (and 300 other people on their Facebook page) about a "new opportunity".

With that being said, here are some jobs to keep far away from:

1.   "Work at Home" Writing Jobs

A lot of these have been appearing lately on Craigslist. The scammer convinces you that there's hundreds of available, decently paying copywriting jobs that you can begin making a lucrative career off of. However, to get access to the list of jobs, you have to pay a one time fee of $70.00. This will send you to a really crappy web platform that doesn't even function.

It's true, there ARE work at home copywriting jobs, and I used to do this exclusively (until I learned better). Companies like Textbroker.com pay about a penny a word, which can add up if you're cranking out a lot every day. Fortunately, you definitely don't have to pay an initial fee to get started. However, it's also not a job for everybody.

2.   Raise Money for Non Profits

Be part of a good cause! Help people out! Save the planet! Congratulations, you're hired!

What they're not telling you is that the reason they have 95% turnover is because the job entails a stiff quota and spamming people on the street to hand over their credit card information (who the hell would do that?). Exceptionally good salespeople can make these jobs work, but I wouldn't waste my time.

3.   WOW! Exciting New Product is Making People MILLIONS

These are called multi-level marketing schemes (MLMs). Although whether they are really a scheme or not is debatable because people have, indeed, made a lot of money selling juice mixers, knife sets, and vitamins of dubious origin.

But to make the real money, you have to sell your soul. First up, you pay THEM an initial "setup fee", and then you're forced to spam all your friends and family members until nobody wants to talk to you ever again.

If you succeed at being a soulless robot, convincing other people to sign up to the same program and also become zombies, you'll start getting kickbacks from other people's setup fees.

It's best just to avoid all this nonsense. I'd rather wash dishes in a hip restaurant.

4.   Google Earns Me Money From Home!

These scams originate in East Europe, in places like Moldova and the Ukraine. The web is filled with these sensational advertisements, and it's merely a ploy to pay for the heroin supply of a one-eyed gangster named Boris.

5.   Make Money Filling Out Surveys!

This is actually something you can try out for fun, but be sure not to use your real e-mail address, and also buy a throwaway phone. I messed around with this for an hour once and made five or six bucks, but the catch is some of the sites they send you to are really sketchy—either containing malware, or they will ask for your phone number as part of the survey, and after entering your digits—you'll start receiving lovely $29.00 monthly phone charges billed to ePharmacyFreeViagraOnlineDiscountDrugstore.com.

If you work with a reputable company, however, the survey thing can be fun if you have nothing better to do.

Honorable Mention: Uber, Lyft and Sidecar: "Be Your Own Boss! Make up to $35.00 an Hour!"

I've seen ads EVERYWHERE recruiting people for the latest app-based transportation companies. As a guy who's been involved in the regular old luxury chauffeur / town-car industry for a couple of years now, I thought I'd weigh in.

I heard that Lyft, the now very popular mustached-car company, fires an extraordinary 94% of their workers. The reason is because they have a mutual employee / customer rating system, and if someone votes you under 5 stars—you're gone.

This is hard considering shit happens in the transportation field—you become late because of a traffic jam, and your client screams bloody murder at you.

So as a quickie job, it's a bad idea because it's not a reliable source of employment. However, I do really enjoy this line of work in the traditional sense—if you have the driving and people skills necessary to make it work.

Chapter 10 – Internet Fallback Jobs

If you did decide to enter a situation of non-employment or a transitory business creation phase, you may be faced with the difficult prospect of needing money to buy groceries and pay bills.

Fortunately, one of the things that first inspired me to write this book is the notion that today, any crafty professional can "fall back" on lower-pay, but reliable, internet contracting jobs to help fill employment gaps.

And, more than a few times people have been known to expand their online presence into a full-time, independent job.

I can't emphasize this enough: **if you can master internet contracting work, you will experience MUCH more peace of mind, especially as it relates to resigning from an employment situation, because you know you'll always have something to fall back on.**

Let's look over some of the major sites:

Fiverr.com (and its many copycat sites)

Cheap job outsourcing through "dollar service jobs" has exploded on the web. I find myself not only participating as a contractor, but using other people's services on Fiverr constantly.

Fiverr consists of five-dollar services, often related to marketing or graphical design type jobs, and options for more experienced contractors to charge a bit more per job. The site keeps $1.00, so you'll earn $4.00 per job.

Some Fiverr jobs boggle my mind, due to their difficulty. Creating original graphic art, for instance, seems a bad deal at $4.00 a pop. The same goes for writing original, lengthy articles for blogs (but people do these types of jobs).

Experts use Fiverr to build services that can be promoted without having to work all day at $2.00 an hour. For instance, some people build huge social media networks and their service is to simply promote a person's website or product to their network. Such a task can be completed in rapid succession.

Textbroker

If you're a good writer, there's a lot of need for copywriters to fill blog posts for companies en masse. Textbroker fulfills that demand, and it's fairly easy to apply and get accepted as a writer.

You'll be assigned a "star ranking" based on how well you write. Most people who write halfway decent get put in the four-star rank. I'm a pretty good writer but even I don't qualify for the five star category, which takes a lot of effort to get into.

At four stars, you make about 1.2 cents per word.

That's not much, like three or four bucks an article, but you can pick what you want to write about, and sometimes you get lucky and find a big project that nets you a large chunk of change. Also, if people really like you, they may start hiring you directly; whereupon you can set your own price.

A downside to Textbroker is nowadays, a lot of people do it, and the jobs disappear pretty fast after they appear on the bulletin board. But, there's also a lot of Textbroker copycat websites if you look around, so you can diversify.

For a while, I made a lot of money solely doing copywriting jobs. It was very handy when I needed supplemental income.

After a while, I found myself burning out on copywriting jobs. But there's a good feeling to know that if I found my income suddenly dropping, I can fall back on sites like Textbroker to keep enough money coming in to keep my head above water.

Elance and Odesk

These are freelance mega-sites for independent contractors to get hired for all manner of jobs. I've diversified my copywriting skills to these sites before, and made pretty good money; at times much better than Textbroker.

The big downside is that it's less reliable to find jobs. Furthermore, they are "race to the bottom" sites where the lowest bidder gets the prize. As a result, the guy in Malaysia who wants to work at $1.00 an hour may be competing with you for a complex graphical design or programming job.

These sites can be beneficial, especially among people who are pretty skilled and need a reliable way to find clients. But at the same time, be careful not to rip yourself off and invest hundreds of hours into something only pays nickels and dimes.

Etsy.com

There's a big community now of DIYers who create their own stuff and sell it on Etsy. A lot of people now feel it's better to support local economies by buying handcrafted instead of shopping at Wal-Mart.

If you're good at knitting sweaters, making arts and craft, or producing your own soap... You might find Etsy is a surprisingly good way to put some food on the table.

Craigslist

At the end of the day, never underestimate the power of Craigslist in your local market to sell your services.

Whatever it is you do, if you post a lot on Craigslist, and keep your eyes peeled for people posting in the community section and seeking help, you can find work.

Just doing copywriting jobs, I've found my best clients on Craigslist. Also, for my videography company, I made most of my big fish clients through posting video service ads in my home city.

Get into a habit of posting a lot on Craigslist. Whatever your skills are, you can market them with some persistence on CL and similar classified ad sites.

In Summary

This is one list, but there are a lot of other service based resources to work online. Keep your eyes open. I've found very well-paying and lesser-known contracting sites.

The challenge is always going to be making a decent salary—especially getting above minimal wage. This can only be done through ingenuity, for instance clever Fiverr gigs or by branding your work as being far more quality; attracting the attention of businesses who want quality over quantity.

By becoming an expert at internet freelance jobs, your confidence level to quit your job will GREATLY increase. It makes a big difference when you know you have stuff to fall back on that doesn't involve flipping hamburgers.

Some people also use these sites as the transition into total independent income.

Closing Chapter

Whether you decided to stay in your job or seek greener fields, I hope that this book at least provided the new perspectives that will help you to understand the importance of taking charge of your finances, and not allowing a job to own you.

We're in the 21st century, and nobody should feel imprisoned by their employment. Furthermore, with so much medical awareness about the danger of stress in the workplace, it should be clear that the benefits a job can provide are NEVER worth it if your blood pressure and peace of mind are continually threatened.

By learning to discover your purpose in life, and developing a winning strategy to turn your most impassioned hobbies into a career, you'll have made the first important steps to following your primary goals in life, whatever it may be. And, perhaps, you can successfully quit your soul-crushing job and find happiness.

(Don't forget, please leave a review on Amazon.com – this will greatly help me make future editions of this book!)

Now, I invite you to view my Amazon author page at **http://www.amazon.com/Cyrus-Kirkpatrick/e/B00LYIV33K/**. Here you can find the rest of the books in the **Cyrus Kirkpatrick Lifestyle Design** series, including titles that are designed to compliment this one, such as:

How to Make Money While Traveling
Freedom: How to Make Money From Your Dreams and Ambitions and *How to Make a Business When You're Broke.*

Working Together

Like what I had to say? Then e-mail me and let's work together. I'm always available for podcasts or even guest writing on blogs. Just drop me a line at cyrus@cyruskirkpatrick.com. You don't have to be an invisible reader, whoever and wherever you are—I want to hear from you.

Free Resources and Freedom Based Work Strategies

If you haven't yet signed up to my CyrusKirkpatrick.com newsletter, then you can do so at www.cyruskirkpatrick.com/subscribe and I'll send you a copy of "11 Steps to a Free Lifestyle", plus weekly tips on lifestyle design.

Other Sites:

Writing as Cyrus Thomson (my middle name) you can find a lot more by me at:

DevelopedLife.com: New concepts in self-development and life coaching, plus a big selection of books.

DevelopedMan.com – Social Intelligence for Men: A men's interest site to deal with some of the social and dating problems we guys face.

That's it for now. I thank you again for purchasing the paperback edition of *How to Quit Your Job*, and I hope that in some way my experiences on this matter will provide a bit of guidance for you, and if this occurs even in some tiny way—then I'll be able to say that creating this book was a successful endeavor.

Until next time,
Cyrus Kirkpatrick

www.ingramcontent.com/pod-product-compliance
Lightning Source LLC
Chambersburg PA
CBHW071244170526
45165CB00003B/1228